INSANELY GREAT
CUSTOMER
SERVICE

*Going beyond ordinary service to unleash
fiercely loyal customer relationships*

by

DANIELLA FAIRBAIRN

CONTENTS

To my parents, my grandparents and my family,

thank you for molding me.

To my mentors, I am eternally grateful.

To my friends, you are my family of choice.

May these words ignite the greatness within.

INSANELY GREAT
CUSTOMER SERVICE

Introduction - Everyone Matters

IN TODAY'S HYPER-busy and overcrowded world, feeling seen and feeling special is more difficult than ever.

It's rare.

But still, it's what we humans crave.

Everyone matters.

Especially when it comes to your customers.

No matter what business you're in, regardless of the industry, you're really in the customer service business at the end of the day.

Everyone matters, whether in healthcare, retail or the restaurant business. Your customer is that client, that patient, that patron, that family member, that friend - anyone who walks through your door or in or around your business. Never underestimate the power of that one person.

The story starts out the same for pretty much everyone.

You go into business for any number of reasons. You may want to exercise your creativity. You may be tired of your boss. You may want to change the world.

But let's face it, you also want to make money.

There's no shame in it. Making money is a pretty essential foundation of business.

No matter what your reasons are for going into business, if you're not making money, your business will not thrive.

That means you can't save the world.

That means you can't exercise your creativity.

That means you might have to go back and rehire your boss.

In order to make that money, though, you need a customer.

And what's more, you need to keep that customer.

Bad customer service makes keeping customers, and, therefore, making money, difficult. It's as simple as that.

The solution is to go on an all-out attack. Attack those bad practices and create new ones. It is no secret that if you are in the service industry, good customer service can be your bread and butter. By providing excellent customer service, you can generate more profit and promote customer loyalty at the same time.

In this book, I'll show you the importance of your interactions with anyone you come across, in any capacity.

Everyone matters.

People may not remember your name; they may not remember all the little details of your product or service, but they remember the way you make them feel. Regardless of the industry – healthcare, dining or retail, it is how you make someone feel that makes them a loyal customer. Taking that extra step to make someone feel comfortable, going the extra mile to make sure the job gets done, this is what keeps people coming back. You never know how a person may be positively affected by your actions; and you never know how a person can positively affect you in return.

Who I Am

I work in health care, something that I've desired to do for the longest. I never wanted a clinical position, but I wanted to make sure that the patient's visit ran smoothly. During a high school internship at a local hospital, I interacted with staff that was very warm and welcoming. Even though I was still a teenager, I felt like an adult in that professional environment. They gave me a sense of responsibility and helped me to realize that as a volunteer, I mattered. I wasn't compensated for my services, but I still mattered. They counted on me, as a volunteer, to work to the best of my ability and to be a helping hand in a fast-paced environment. I learned how to take blood pressures, how to take accurate weights, and temperatures. I knew there was something more, and if I wanted to be the best that I could be, I had to emulate someone who excelled in her position. The Nurse Manager for that particular department served as a mentor. She was friendly, warm, diligent, and made it very clear how hard she worked to get to that level. She never appeared to have a bad day and maintained her professionalism at all times.

I also recall my experience as a summer camp assistant. I worked in the business office with administrators;

making sure that the phones were answered, accepting applications, checking their completion status and other administrative duties. Again, I was a teenager, but I felt like an adult. I took pride in my work, and I really enjoyed it. In fact, it became more than just working at the summer camp. It evolved into work in-between my school breaks and helping the administrators at a moment's notice. I was embraced in that environment, something that is forever etched in my memory.

Regardless of the experience, going above and beyond has always been second-nature. Nonetheless, there were several values that I took from my professional career – friendliness, humility, approachability, and efficiency.

This particular book is my thank you. It's my thank you to my mentors who over the years have led me on the path of greatness. Recently, I attended an event in which Les Brown was the keynote speaker. He stated, "Mentors are those who see the best in you." You may not foresee your destiny, but they're the one person who sees greatness within you. I am eternally grateful.

In turn, I've always enjoyed bringing out the best in someone. I particularly love working behind the scenes, just to make sure those at the forefront have the best presentation. That's always brought me joy.

Whenever things are in disarray, it makes me tingle just to think that I can possibly turn this into something better. When I walk into a room, my eyes start to dance as I look around and take note of the smallest details.

I recall auditioning for major drama in junior high school which was definitely out of my comfort zone, as I'm very reserved by nature. Funny enough, I passed the audition and immediately came up with my master plan of doing everything other than acting.

I wanted to make sure that the actors were set with costume and props; becoming stage manager by default. I took copious notes during class and led those in black behind the scenes, always moving things into place so that voila, when the curtain opened, everything just magically appeared.

Structure and organization. That was my objective since my earlier years, and I realized throughout life that stage management was my passion.

I think this ability definitely stems from my formative years. I'm a daddy's girl, the eldest of three, and I remember my father saying "Dede, you are in charge. Look after your sister and brother." There wasn't much of an age difference between my siblings and me, but it was having that sense of responsibility at a young age that enabled me to stay focused and take care of them. It also translated into my work and my friendships as I was often the grounded one in the group, often laying out the possibilities and thinking about the next steps.

Being a stage manager in health care is an exhilarating experience. It's making sure that, upon arrival, a person feels at home – that they always matter. Whether they are a client, whether they are a patient, whether they are a co-worker, whether they are a vendor, everyone matters.

There are tangible benefits to better serving your customer. Among these are increased revenue, increased profit, and increased market share. But there are are also less tangible benefits. It's about someone's feelings; how you particularly make that customer feel. Imagine feeling one way upon arrival, and then feeling uplifted upon departure. It's about making someone feel good about themselves. Making them feel safe whenever they enter your space. Businesses that report high levels of customer satisfaction almost never struggle. Take a business like Whole Foods for example. I'm sure you've heard countless people complain about their prices and how expensive everything is. Yet they're doing better than ever, opening a new store every five minutes it seems.

Why?

The answer to this is simple. They take good customer service seriously. They can justify their higher prices because, at the end of the day, customers will keep coming back to get that unique experience that they offer. This is what differentiates them from all the other supermarkets out there.

If you follow these steps and the advice in this book, you too will enjoy happier customers and more money.

You Can't Afford To Wait

Nowadays, a new business starts up every second. Because of this, it gets harder and harder to differentiate. Harder and harder to stand out; to cut through all the noise. You simply can't afford to take your customer service practices lightly. If you don't differentiate now, someone else will come along and steal your customers from right under your nose.

CHAPTER 1 - THE SEARCH FOR GOOD CUSTOMER SERVICE

HAS THIS EVER Happened To You?

You call up your doctor's office to make an appointment. If you're lucky you may get one right away or within a few days. But it's also not uncommon to have to wait several weeks for your doctor's office to have an available slot for you.

Assuming you've waited awhile for your appointment, you no doubt want to make sure that you show up to the office on time so that you can be seen right away.

So you show up and then...nothing.

The receptionist checks you in, tells you to have a seat, and then you wait.

And wait.

And wait.

It seems like everyone gets to see the doctor before you, even the people that arrived after you did.

And when you try to get more information, what are you usually told?

"The doctor will see you soon. Please have a seat and wait."

You can end up waiting for any number of hours in the healthcare facility for a visit.

I don't know about you, but that's something that drives me nuts.

If my appointment is at one o'clock, why can't I be seen at one o'clock? Or even within a half hour of one o'clock?

In general, it can be difficult to fit even a doctor's appointment into our busy schedules. Sometimes, you have to take off work or rush to the office after work. After all this, I just want to feel as if I'll be attended to right away. I also want to make sure that I'm made privy to anything that may cause a delay.

In grad school, as a part of my final project, I conducted focus groups at a community health center. Most of the time, the participants actually just wanted to know what was happening. If their appointment was at twelve o'clock, why did they have to wait until three o'clock, for instance, to be seen? It was the lack of communication that was most frustrating.

Several years ago, my grandfather fell ill and was admitted to the hospital for several weeks. At first, no one seemed sure of his prognosis. But later, a doctor confirmed that my grandfather experienced symptoms of dementia.

It was something that was very scary for us, and we wanted to handle it properly. My grandfather was a very proud strong man, and to see him this way really threw me for a loop.

There were times when he would say 'don't say anything to the staff here...don't complain about anything, because at night, they'd get me'. Now I didn't know if that was true because, again, he was experiencing dementia. But still there seemed to be no recourse in rectifying the situation. There was no signage. It wasn't clear who I would speak to about our questions. And there was little transparency. What really took place after hours? Who could we talk to? That was frustrating for me. It was frustrating for my family. We wanted to make sure that my grandfather was taken care of, and we wanted to know who we could turn to.

When someone enters an establishment, whether it's a healthcare facility or dining establishment, or a retail store, they should feel comfortable in that instant. As you know, first impressions say a lot.

The other day, I needed a prescription and I spoke with my doctor. In that moment of calling the doctor, he was very amicable, as he usually is, and we were able to get what we needed done.

Afterwards, I had to call the pharmacy, and that's where things got complicated. I spoke with the front desk person, and she wanted to know what pharmacy I'd been to before. She wanted to make sure that when she called the pharmacy that they were able to fill the prescription, which was perfectly fine.

But it didn't come out that way. Instead, it came across like she didn't have time to call different pharmacies. It bothered me because I was the client in this situation.

I should not feel rushed. I should not feel pressured.

At the time, I was driving, and I wasn't able to pull over to look up the phone number. When I did finally respond to her, it was in a somewhat negative way because I felt she wasn't helpful enough.

And you can see how it all turns into a vicious cycle from there.

Bottom line, a customer should not feel as if they are bothering someone by simply asking them to do their job.

We've all experienced it.

And how does it make you feel? Do you feel like you want to continue giving that particular establishment your business?

Probably not.

And that is exactly how your customers feel when they receive bad service from your business.

What All This Has To Do With You

Everyone is vying for a customer's attention. Everyone is trying to sell something to the same people.

There are only so many dollars to go around, and so customers have to pick and choose. Plus, consumers are savvier than ever before.

How do you make yourself seem better? How do you make your business stand out?

What You're Really Selling

First, you have to realize that you're not selling whatever it is you think you're selling.

Stay with me here.

Let's say you're in the corn on the cob business.

You're not really selling that corn on the cob.

You're selling an idea, the idea that the corn on the cob represents.

What you're really doing is selling the customer on their own worldview, their view of themselves. Or of the self they desire to be.

That's the story of Justin Gignac, the creator of www.nycgarbage.com and the guy who set out to prove that you could sell anything with the right packaging.

Justin roams the streets of New York City, gathering used cigarette butts, old yogurt cups, dirty diapers, used matches, and all sorts of useless garbage you can imagine. Then, he brings it all back to his studio, packages it into a clear plastic box that reads, "Garbage of New York City," signs it and then sells each one for up to $100 a pop.

He's even got some limited edition collections, like garbage that includes items from President Obama's campaign.

Why do you think people buy it?

Why would anyone buy trash?

Garbage? Filth?

Because he piggybacks off of the draw of New York City, and all it represents.

Were this trash curated from Arkansas, would it have been as successful? Probably not.

But rather, when you buy a cube of New York City trash, it represents something. What it represents is the key here, because while most people may be inclined to suggest it represents freedom (The Statue of Liberty), creativity (it's art! and trash! and art!), or dreams (if you can make it here...), none of those answers help explain why folks would be lining up out the door to buy them.

Why wouldn't they just draw themselves a little Statue of Liberty on their notebook and be done with it?

What it really represents is something much greater than all of that.

What it really represents? Is that person's identity. And what kind of a statement they're making about the person they are.

This is powerful stuff.

Make your customer feel seen and their wallets will subsequently open.

TAKE I

What's your story?

- What's your passion?
- Why did you get involved in this business?
- What's your product?

Think of your elevator pitch. How would you sum up your business in 30 seconds?

Daniella Fairbairn

NOTES:

TAKE II

Who's Your Customer?

Internal Customer	External Customer
1.	1.
2.	2.
3.	3.
4.	4.
5.	5.

How would your customers describe you?

Internal Customer	External Customer
1.	1.
2.	2.
3.	3.
4.	4.
5.	5.

Chapter 2 - How The Very First Customer Was Born

WE WEREN'T ALWAYS the high-tech, uber-civilized society we are today.

Quiet as it's kept, we used to be pretty basic.

Eat when hungry. Sleep when tired.

We lived in small, familial groups, wearing animal furs. We hunted and foraged for our food.

Necessity dictated that we move around a lot. We needed to go wherever the food was.

Discovering fire helped us out tremendously as a civilization, but we were about to make another discovery that would dramatically and irrevocably change the game.

With the advent of agriculture, we no longer had to constantly move around and hunt buffalo. We could stay in one place, dig up some dirt, plant some seeds, and food would magically appear from the ground.

This was nothing short of revolutionary.

So much so that it was called the agricultural revolution.

Families could be larger (and in fact needed to be larger because we needed bodies to work the land).

We didn't have to move from place to place unless we wanted to.

And another critical byproduct of all this was something called the specialization of skills.

Communities began to form. We, in turn, built and made things that sustained those communities. And in the process, some people became really good at some things, making shoes for example. While others became really good at other things, like making beer.

If you made a killer brew but didn't know a thing about shoes, maybe you could take some of your fine ale down the road and see if the resident shoemaker would be up for an exchange.

And thus, the very first customers were born.

If you were the only shoemaker in your area, then you had a built-in and captive clientele. People had no choice but to come to you.

But then cities and towns began to form. And as a result, transportation was revolutionized.

Other shoemakers could now crop up nearby. Or at least near enough to travel to. People won't have to come to you anymore. They can hop in a horse and buggy and visit the shoemaker the next town over.

So how do you hold onto your customer?

You need to have a value proposition that's better than the other shoemaker's. Maybe his shoe is better quality. But let's say that your wife bakes the meanest apple bread for miles to come. And your repeat customers go home with not only a snazzy new pair of shoes but a warm loaf of bread as well. Maybe you offer foot rubs while customers wait to be measured.

Are you getting my drift?

These are the beginnings of customer service as a concept, acknowledging that a person doesn't have to spend their money with you, and coming up with ways to make them choose you over your competition.

While we're on the subject of shoes, I love over the knee boots. Usually, I shop at the same boutique every year to get them. The boutique owner makes me feel great when I walk into his store. We joke, we have conversations. It's an amazing feeling. In this place, I never feel rushed, they always have my size, and they also have the width that I need for my calves.

 I don't have to go anywhere else.

I went in one day and said to myself that I was not going to spend more than $100 on a new pair of boots. I was definitely about to go over budget because I saw a pair of boots that I really liked. They looked good and were on trend. I didn't mind spending a little extra because I wanted to treat myself. I also mentioned to the boutique owner that the pair of boots that I bought the previous year were actually damaged because I wore them in the snow when I wasn't supposed to.

He said, *"Why don't you just bring them back? I'll give them to you for the same price it would cost me to repair them."* Can you guess how good that made me feel? Even though I didn't live nearby, I wanted to go right back to get the damaged boots and come back for the exchange. All because I felt comfortable with the boutique owner and I knew the quality of shoes that he'd sold to me in the past.

So why not take that extra step? Why not go the extra mile?

It could mean the difference between a lifelong customer and someone who's "just looking."

TAKE III

Why are you here?

- To Show Customers You Care
- To Get Team Buy-In
- To Diagnose Your Customers Needs
- To Best Respond to Customer Requests

	TODAY	IDEALLY
How do you show customers you care?		
How do you get team buy-in?		
How do you diagnose customer needs?		
How do you respond to customer qustions?		

Daniella Fairbairn

NOTES:

Chapter 3 - The Most Common Types of Difficult Customers and How To Deal With Them

IN BUSINESS, YOU can expect to come across difficult customers on an almost daily basis. Dealing with difficult customers can be upsetting and draining and damaging to your team morale. But if we understand ahead of time, who our difficult customers are and come up with effective strategies for dealing with them, we can feel much more empowered when those situations do arise.

In fact, there are several types of difficult customers.

They are:

• **The "Yes Man" or "Yes Woman"** – These are the customers that will "yes" you to death. They are uncomfortable saying no, so they will either avoid you or they will agree to things they don't really want to agree to.

Tips for dealing with this customer type - You need to make the environment as low pressure as possible. Ask questions to get to the bottom of what this customer really wants and then deliver just that; nothing more and nothing less.

• **The Church Mouse** – Not everyone is good at being assertive and voicing their opinion. This customer type tends to be quieter and more passive. They aren't good at asking questions, and so if you are not ready to greet them and make them feel at ease, you could lose sales.

Tips for dealing with this customer type - Make them comfortable. Cultivate a genuine connection. Observe them so that you can anticipate their needs and deliver, without them having to ask.

• **The Quintessential Bully** – We've all encountered a bully at some point. These customers are the ones that can't seem to be helped no matter what you do. They always have harsh words and are always trying to manipulate a situation by making others feel badly.

Tips for dealing with this customer type - In life, the best way to deal with a bully is usually to stand up to them. In business, things are a bit different. You don't want to engage and stoop to this customer's level. You want to control your attitude and reaction. Being anything less than professional will only make the situation worse. If things get really out of hand, excuse yourself and get a manager or supervisor.

• **The "Not Now" Type** – This customer type can seem quite indecisive. They don't commit. They don't make a decision.

Tips for dealing with this customer type - The trick here is to realize that if this customer type isn't ready to make a decision, it's more than likely because they don't want the product or service at that time. Don't pressure them. That will only put them off. Reinforce what makes the product or service great, show some social proof, and then give this customer plenty of breathing room to come around on his or her own. Forcing the issue will almost always result in a no. One trick is to anticipate any objections the customer may raise and have an answer ready.

• **The "Knows Everything" Type** – Some customers will make it seem that they are better at your job than you are. They're not, of course, but they certainly seem to think so.

Tips for dealing with this customer type - Don't argue and stick to the facts. Nod politely and get them what they need as quickly as possible.

• The "Can't Get No Satisfaction" Type – Some people are just never happy despite our best efforts. This customer type is one that always seems to have a complaint.

Tips for dealing with this customer type - Appease the customer with some reward. Make sure policies and such are clearly stated. Make sure you have an answer ready for any potential negatives they could bring up.

TAKE IV: Personality Types

Based on the personality type, know how to identify your customers quickly.

1. Which of the four personality types – red, yellow, blue, green – best describes you when you are the consumer? Why?

RED DIRECTOR	YELLOW RELATOR
• *Strengths:* Administration, taking initiative.	• *Strengths:* Servicing, listening.
• *Weaknesses:* Impatience, insensitivity.	• *Weakness:* Oversensitivity, indecision.
• *Goals:* Productivity, control.	*Goals:* Acceptance, Stability
• *Fear:* Being hustled.	• *Fear:* Sudden change.
• *Motivator:* Winning.	• *Motivator:* Involvement.
• *Irritation:* Indecision.	• *Irritation:* Insensitivity.

BLUE SOCIAL	GREEN THINKER/ ANALYZER
• *Strengths:* Persuasion, interaction w/ others.	• *Strengths:* Planning, analyzing.
• *Weaknesses:* Disorganization, carelessness.	• *Weakness:* Perfectionists, critical.
• *Goals:* Popularity, applause.	• *Goals:* Accuracy, thoroughness.
• *Fear:* Loss of prestige.	• *Fear:* Criticism.
• *Motivator:* Recognition.	• *Motivator:* Progress.
• *Irritation:* Routine.	• *Irritation:* Unpredictability.

2. What do you think difficult customers get out of their inappropriate behavior? Pick two types and explain.

3. Think of a recent customer scenario that didn't go well. What type of customer were they? What could you have done differently to deal with them more effectively?

NOTES:

Chapter 4 - Poor Customer Service: What It Looks Like and How To Avoid It

WHAT IS POOR Customer Service?

We talked briefly about your customer's worldview, their view of themselves, and the importance of making them feel seen.

When most people think about poor customer service, they think of the extremes; downright rude and disrespectful and even abusive behavior.

I challenge you to think deeper than that.

Poor customer service certainly does encompass the above and also so much more. Poor customer service, in essence, is anything that doesn't make your customer feel seen. Or feel heard. Or feel understood. Anything that doesn't make your customer feel like a priority.

Poor customer service doesn't discriminate. No business, regardless of the industry, is exempt from it.

What does it look like?

Let's take a look at the common instances of poor customer service. There are many, many ways that poor customer service can show up in your business. These are just a few:

-Not making eye contact

-Not answering a customer's question

-Refusing to acknowledge mistakes

Below are just some of the things that frustrate your customers:

-Having to talk to multiple people and starting over everytime

-Being made to wait

-Not getting what's needed on the first try

-Dealing with a rude or inexperienced representative

-Difficulty navigating a website

-Frequent service interruptions

Now when you dine out, you want to feel as if you're spending your money where you're wanted. There may be times when you go into an establishment, and you are looking forward to a great experience. What if, upon stepping into the establishment, you were not acknowledged in any way? What if there was a long wait and no update as to what was happening? What if you had to seat yourself or wait a long time to be attended to?

If you take a sip of your drink and you don't like it, will you be able to get another drink and not be charged? Do you want to hear that there are no exchanges as per the restaurant's policy?

Of course not.

What Are Some Of The Causes of Poor Customer Service?

But why does this happen?

Why do some people experience poor customer service rather than great customer service?

Bad Product - You can be as nice as you could possibly

be. If your product or service is not quality, then can you really say you've served your customers?

Not Knowing Your Market - This goes back to making your customer feel seen. When you know who your customer is and what it is they really want, then you can create a product or service that speaks specifically to that, as opposed to just selling them what you think they need or want.

Ineffective Hiring - Are you properly screening your candidates? Are you hiring people just because you need a body? Or are you taking the time to make sure you get the best possible people for the job? Most of your customer service woes can be eliminated right at the very beginning, during the hiring process.

Poor Training - OK so let's say you've hired the perfect candidates, and you're feeling good. Do you just throw them into the lake and hope that they'll learn to swim? Or do you take the time to properly train them to do the job the way you want it done? Keep in mind that training isn't something that's just done the first week or two on the job. Training is an ongoing process.

Unclear Expectations - Do your employees even know that providing excellent customer service is a part of their job description? Are they being held accountable when they don't meet these expectations?

Disengaged Management - If excellent customer service practices are not being modeled at the management level, you can hardly expect your employees to follow suit.

What Are The Effects of Poor Customer Service?

When a customer has a bad experience with your business, any number of things can and will happen. Among these are:

1. **They tell other people about it** - This is huge. Word of mouth is a very powerful thing. We've all experienced the phenomenon that is social media. All it takes is one tweet, one bad Yelp review, one Facebook comment, to drag your business' name through the mud. Public shaming is a very real thing. Don't let your business be the next victim of an internet takedown.

2. **They ask for a supervisor or manager** - This then cuts into the manager's time and workload and is often followed up with disciplinary action.

3. **They submit negative reviews** - Reviews are increasingly how consumers choose which business they patronize. A potential new customer could have been all

set to walk through your doors, but then, after reading negative reviews, changed their mind. More than 60 percent of consumers are influenced by other consumer's comments about companies – word of mouth can quickly destroy the reputation of a company.

4. They write a complaint letter - This will often result in your boss's boss getting in trouble. Complaint letters have a way of finding the highest ranks within the company, and that type of negativity can only roll downhill.

5. They cease doing business with the company - This results in lost revenue. Enough lost revenue can result in your company going into debt or eventually having to close its doors. The job of any responsible business owner is to stay in the black.

The Myth Of The "Bad Day"

Your attitude should not have an effect on your work. One bad day should not equate to zero dollars. For those on the front line that may be the first point of contact in a business or establishment or facility, you play a significant role in what happens next.

There may be a service that someone needs. There may be an item that they want. You are how they get to that particular item. And because you are that front line person, it's important that you do the ground work. It's important that you lay the foundation. And in anything that you do, a strong foundation enables one to stand firm.

Saying that you're having a bad day or saying that's how you are, is not good enough.

We all have bad days.

Your customers have bad days. Consider the possibility that the day they're having is actually worse than yours.

It may sound harsh, but the truth is that no one wants to hear about your headache. No one wants to hear that you haven't yet had a break.

As employees, and adults, we're expected to learn how to adapt to adversity and power through it.

That's the reality.

So no more "bad days."

TAKE V

"You're only as good as your team"

Step-by-Step Plan for Team Building

- Recruit the best
- Understand your mission and vision
- Share your values
- Focus on strengths
- Groom your leaders

Step 1 - Prepare materials and tools for customer service training.

Be as detailed and specific as you can when composing materials for customer service training. It is imperative that your employees understand what you think good customer service should be. Give them concrete examples of acceptable and unacceptable behavior. Provide them with a list of do's and don'ts to remember.

Secondly, help them understand why offering good customer service is important to the business and how it will ultimately affect them as well. Employees will be more motivated to improve their customer service skills if they believe that doing so is beneficial to them as well.

Prepare scripts for common customer service issues. This will ensure that your customer service team will be able to deliver a speedy and uniform response to your customers. Determine your desired response schedule and make sure that the training materials are designed to help them comply with the desired response time.

Step 2 - Take all the time you need to train your staff.

Focus on one lesson at a time and don't progress to another level until you're sure they've mastered their lessons. It is a good idea to hold periodic tests to ensure that they continue to retain knowledge from your previous lessons.

Let them take a gradual approach to their new set of responsibilities. Have them start with something small and relatively easy like handling routine customer service calls. Always clarify their job duties and the level of authority they're working with before allowing them to interact with the customers.

Last, but not the least, remind them to consult your FAQ section before delving into more complicated processes of resolution.

Step 3 - Monitor the performance of your customer service team.

Subject your employees to scheduled and spontaneous simulations to give you a chance to evaluate their response in critical situations. Make sure that you provide feedback afterwards; identifying their strengths, weaknesses and offering suggestions for improvement.

You may even consider developing an incentive program to further motivate your employees and encourage them to always be at their best when interacting with customers. It is also important to evaluate your employee's customer service abilities on a regular basis.

Last, but not the least, always be prepared to make changes with how you run your customer service team. Remember they directly interact with your customers, so your team and its policies must be flexible in order to respond quickly to a customer's needs.

Make your customer service training more effective with creative and fun customer service training games.

CHAPTER 5 - GOOD CUSTOMER SERVICE: WHAT IT LOOKS LIKE AND HOW TO GET IT

WHAT IS GOOD Customer Service?

This all begs the question, what does good customer service actually mean and how do we achieve it?

We know that good customer service is essential. But if you ask ten people what good customer service means to them, you'll surely get ten entirely different answers.

To some, good customer service is as simple as solving problems and offering solutions promptly. To others, it means overall pleasantness and politeness from those who represent the front lines of a company.

Others define it as when a company is willing to give their customers anything and everything that they want -- you know, the customer is always right approach - no matter how unreasonable some of those demands may be.

There isn't a right or a wrong because the factors of what makes customer service "good" also depend heavily upon what specific things a particular customer may hold valuable or their expectations from what industry competitors do.

Good customer service is partly defined by the industry, but a large part of how your company defines good customer service will determine what good customer service means to you.

However, there are definitely customer service basics you should be covering. These factors may seem simple, but actually implementing them in your business may take more strategy, time, and effort to achieve a truly satisfying customer experience.

Again, always remember that we want the customer to feel seen.

What does it look like?

Let's take a look at the common features of good customer service. Good customer service may show up in your business as:

-Greetings upon entering your establishment

-Making eye contact while talking

-Remembering customer names

-Offering special orders and services

-Customer appreciation practices

-Being present and genuinely helpful

-Being in a good mood and being polite

Take for instance a family owned restaurant that has been around the neighborhood for over seventy years, where lines often extend around the corner every weekend. The owner once told me, 'it's all about the way you treat people'. While patrons, waiting in line, in the cold, to go into this restaurant they are offered tea, they are offered cookies, they are offered juice, they are offered fruit, and once they actually enter the establishment, they are treated like family. And once they order, the food comes out quickly. There's never a delay so people don't mind the wait time.

When you think of customers, and you look at these businesses, the customers will tell you how they feel about it, and they don't mind doing something that they wouldn't ordinarily do just to get the service that they are looking for.

I heard a great story recently about a gentleman who went to a new supermarket for the first time. He was looking for a particular type of bread and didn't know where to find it. The employee went with him to the aisle and showed him where to find what he was looking for. She even explained the differences between the various types of bread. And, as if that wasn't enough, she gave him a tour when she found out it was his first visit.

What Are Some Of The Causes of Good Customer Service?

Good Hiring Practices - Taking the time to properly screen candidates and ask thoughtful interview questions are hugely important steps in the selection process. You have to start out with the right people. If you do, half the job of creating a culture of good service is already done.

Good and Ongoing Training - Once your new hires are in the door, you're going to need to hold their hands for a bit. It's an inescapable part of things. Give the written material with expectations clearly spelled out.

Show company training videos. Have one-on-one sessions with them and model desired behaviors. You simply cannot overdo this part. The more training, the better. That goes for ongoing training as well. Everyone, even the absolute best employees, needs refreshers and reminders every now and again.

Clear Expectations and Company Culture - Your employees need to know that providing good service is a fundamental part of their jobs. This should be an overall part of your company's culture.

Feedback and Accountability - Feedback is essential. Employees need to know what they're good at and what they need to improve. If the service an employee provides is not up to standard, tell him. If the issue is ongoing, then you need to have systems in place for holding him accountable. This sends a clear message about what will and will not be tolerated in your business.

What Are The Effects of Good Customer Service?

When a customer has a positive experience with your business, any number of things can and will happen. Among these are:

1. **Telling other people about it** - When a customer has

a positive experience with your business, it's like free advertising for you.

2. **Submitting positive reviews** - In general, happy customers will reward you with more customers. You can't help but grow your business when customers are happy.

3. **Sending complimentary emails** - The positive and momentum-building effects of a complimentary letter or email cannot be understated. When people know that their hard work is noticed and appreciated, they want to do more of it.

4. **Purchasing additional products and services** - This all leads to an increased customer base and increased revenue. It's also important to remember that it costs less money to retain an existing customer than it does to convert a new one altogether.

What To Do When You Receive A Customer Complaint

Never leave issues unresolved. Every complaint must be successfully addressed. Train your employees to perform follow-up calls to ensure that all complaints have been addressed. For complicated issues, make sure that you give customers progress reports to let them know that you're still working on their case. Do your best to give them a specific time period for which they can expect the issue to be fully resolved.

Take Responsibility - Acknowledge that you were in the wrong. Nothing is more frustrating to a customer than when they bring up a grievance and are made to feel that the incident is actually their fault. Everyone makes mistakes. Take ownership.

Apologize - Let the customer know you're sorry. Let them know that this is not what your business is about and that this was a one-off mistake. Apologize sincerely.

Fix It - Take steps to correct the mistake. If a solution doesn't readily present itself, ask the customer what they would like or what you can do to fix it.

Prevent Further Mistakes From Happening - Don't you hate when someone apologizes to you and then continues to do the same thing over and over again? If a customer addresses the same mistake frequently, they will start to question the sincerity of your apology. Find the root of the error and deal with it. Hold the responsible persons accountable to help prevent any future occurrences.

TAKE VI

Phone Etiquette
"A First Impression is a Lasting One"

GOOD PHONE ETIQUETTE	POOR PHONE ETIQUETTE
May I place you on hold?	Hold on.
Good _____, thank you for calling _____. This is _____. How may I help you?	Name of Business.
I'll check for you right away.	I don't know.
Certainly/Very Well.	No Problem/Okay.

NOTES:

TAKE VII

"It's not what you say, but how you say it"

Scripts for challenging customers

Scenario I: Disengaged member of the team

Scenario II: Customer is dissatisfied with product

Scenario III: Customer is unhappy with service

CHAPTER 6 - CREATING A CULTURE OF GREAT SERVICE

PUT YOURSELF IN Your Customer's Shoes

The little things are what matters. It's not necessarily about big names. If you don't mind spending the extra dollar for quality, that means someone else will want to do the same. And so why not provide quality? Why not go the extra mile? Why not make somebody feel good about herself?

You know exactly how you would like to feel when you walk into a place of business. Build from there. Offer information. Anticipate a customer's needs. Be available as much as possible. Get to know your customers. These are all factors that you should consider when you are thinking about customer service improvement and what needs to happen in your business.

An Ounce Of Prevention…

The absolute best way to combat the issue of poor customer service in your business is to do everything you can to prevent it from happening in the first place.

Here are the various ways you can do just that:

Know Your Customer - Do you know your customer? I mean really know them. This goes beyond knowing their basic demographics. Get to know your customer on a more intimate level. If you know what drives them, if you know what they fear, then you'll know how to provide what they need.

How do you get to know your customers better?

Listen to them. Do you make a hasty excuse and hang up when they start to ramble? Would it kill you to listen and be present to them for a few minutes longer?

Observe them. Do they always buy the same thing when they come to your establishment or are they always trying something different? Is there a particular staff member they seem drawn to? Are they purchasing just for themselves or do they have a family? Make note of your customers' individual quirks and preferences. It's valuable information you can use to serve them better.

Ask them. Is there a feedback system in place in your

business? Do your customers know how to get in contact with someone if they have a question or concern? Make sure this information is prominently displayed.

Start With Awesome - Having what the customer wants in the first place is the most fundamental form of customer service. Your product or your service simply must be awesome. It has to be something that solves a problem or fills a need. Either that or it has to be something cutting edge and not easily resisted. All the great customer service practices in the world won't help if your product is not awesome. Take some time to develop this aspect of your business first.

Show Up - The majority of providing good customer service is simply just showing up. When someone needs help with something are you available? Can you help them find the answer to their question? If not, can you take them to the person that can?

Company Culture - Great customer service starts from the top. It shouldn't be an afterthought or a bullet point but rather something you instill in your employees from the very first day. It should be a major part of the overall culture you're creating in your business. You do this starting with your hiring practices, and then orientations and training, and finally with accountability and feedback.

Measure and Keeps Tabs - You're not in the trenches all of the time. You can't be. So how do you measure your customer's experience and keep tabs on the people you've hired to represent your brand? There are a couple of ways. You can employ the use of secret shoppers. And you can make use of customer feedback forms.

Training Staff

Staff communication is vital to the success of any business. Failure to communicate can set off a   loss of valuable human capital. After all, who doesn't want to be informed of their company's updates?

Here are some helpful tips when communicating with your employees:

Prepare earlier - Before carrying out communications with your staff, please note all points of discussion beforehand. Trust me, you'll be better able to explain everything in the clearest manner possible.

Present complete information - Provide complete and accurate information to your employees. Confidential information need not be shared, but it is important that you give them all the necessary points.

Plan for a regular meeting - It is essential to plan meetings on a regular basis to keep the employees updated on organizational goals and policies. Such meetings will also help to enhance the manager/ employee relationship. But when you plan your meetings, be careful not to plan them too frequently as they may lose their value. Therefore, planned periodic meetings held at sufficiently long intervals will help to maintain normal communication plans.

Keep your meetings brief - While it is important that you provide all essential information to your employees, do not prolong the conversation as it is best to maximize utilization of the available work time for employee productivity. Long meetings can also minimize the incentive for employees.

Assign responsibilities and form proper teams - When you hand over jobs to your employees, it is advisable to assign responsibilities to select, efficient employees in order to streamline communications. Such an organized manner of communication will also ensure that complaints are addressed by another party in your absence.

Create faith in your employees - A trusted relationship will help improve motivation among your employees. It is important that you become a trusted communicator to get the maximum output and efficiency from your employees. Also, show your employees that you trust them. This will help to create confidence in your staff.

Listen to your staff - It is not only important that you communicate efficiently; you also need to listen carefully. Listening to your staff is part of the effective communication process. Unless you understand and sort out the complaints, you will not be able to inspire them.

Convey your expectations - You have to express what you expect from your employees. It is better to talk to them about long term and short term goals rather than encourage rising expectations. It is wise to sit and discuss goals and abilities to avoid future disappointments.

Determining the best strategies and methodologies for communication is essential for the longevity of your business. Not only is productivity affected, but profits are as well.

Getting Customer Feedback

One thing all customers have in common is the pleasure they receive when establishments that they patronize make it clear to them that they know who they all are.

Make good use of FAQ's. If you don't have a frequently asked questions file or web page for your business, create one immediately. Having an FAQ page is an effective way of offering good customer service on the fly. Keep a record of common questions and problems that have been discussed for quick reference. This will help to negate the need for repeat calls regarding the same issues. FAQ sections can help prevent your customers and employees from wasting their time.

Conduct thorough customer service surveys, where positive and negative remarks are clearly shown. This information allows the business to evaluate their standards and develop better customer service policies. Customer service surveys can also help when it comes to making good business decisions.

A well-written customer survey can give you all of the information that you need to make positive changes for your business. On the other hand, surveys that aren't well-written will not help you achieve the results that you want. To avoid this, it is important that you follow a few simple guidelines to craft an effective questionnaire:

Identify your objectives - The survey objectives are crucial. Carefully identify your specific objectives. When goals are not clear, you will end up with a questionnaire that is unfocused and ineffective. Always be direct about the information you want to acquire. Successful surveys act as tools in denying and confirming the customer's expectation from your business.

Questions in the survey must be easily answered - Customers don't want to have a hard time answering your questions. Never use abbreviations, slang or any technical jargon in your questionnaire. You will obtain more helpful answers if you make the questions easy.

Alternate your questions - Try mixing easy and difficult questions throughout your survey. This will help keep the customers interested and encourage them to answer more questions. A good rule of thumb is to set two easy questions first, like the "yes" or "no" and the multiple choice questions. Then start to include your open-ended questions. This process will keep your customers from feeling like you are requesting too much from them.

Don't be biased - Lastly, don't make the questions biased. Successful surveys should get the true opinion of the customer and not just the answers that you want to hear. This is the best way to measure customer satisfaction.

When it comes to crafting a good survey you can use

different types of questions, such as:

-Questions answered with a simple yes or no.
(i.e. *Will you purchase this product again?*)

-Questions answered by multiple choice.
(i.e. *Which products do you like most? Product A, B, or C?*)

-Scale or rankings and ask the customer to rate their experience. (i.e. *Please rate our service from 1 to 5*)

-Use open-ended questions.
(i.e. *What are your suggestions to better improve our services?*)

Customer service surveys are a very important tool that can help you make informed decisions for the betterment of your business, products and services. If your goal is to achieve a 100% satisfaction rating from your customers, surveys will definitely help you to achieve that goal.

TAKE VIII

Benefits of Excellent Service

"Do Unto Others As You Would Have Done Unto You"

Eight Customer Service Essentials
1. Know Your Team
2. Transparency
3. Ask Questions
4. Appreciate your customers
5. Find ways to help your customers
6. Humility
7. Anticipate your customer's needs
8. Feedback

NOTES:

Conclusion - It All Starts From The Top

ANYONE CAN TELL people what to do, tell them what's expected of them.

It takes a truly special person to live it and demonstrate it.

Will you model the behaviors you want to see in your staff? Can you have the tough conversations when people aren't performing up to standard? Can you be consistent and hold everyone accountable across the board.

Will you be a conscious leader?

It all starts from the top.

Let's go over a few simple secrets that you can use for your own business.

Strive to build customer loyalty - Customer loyalty is the most important factor in achieving good customer service. Do your best to collect your customer's full name, contact numbers and other information. Remember if you show concern for what matters to your customers, you will build their loyalty and have that customer for life.

Provide authentic customer service - It's high time that you personalize your service. Be creative. Personally know your customers and identify their individual needs. Make certain that you offer extreme value to your customers.

The customer is always right - The old adage "the customer is always right" is still applicable. If a customer approaches you and complains, be serious when handling the concern. If the customer is angry and upset, do your best to defuse the situation and show them how serious you are when it comes to correcting any problems. Once the customer is satisfied with how you address their complaint, thank them for conveying the problem. Keep in mind that advertisement will not be enough to repair a damage done by failing to address customer complaints. Silent complainers can do a great deal of damage to your business. Beware of people who walk away without having their issue resolved. You may never see them again. If they are unhappy, you can bet that they are openly criticizing your services to other people and creating a bad reputation for your business.

Be honest with the customers - Once your customer suspects that you are lying to them, they are a lost buyer. If a customer seeks your advice about a product, openly tell them what they need to know. In the end, they will thank you for being so genuine with what you offer.

Go the extra mile - If you want superb customer service, you should always go the extra mile. For instance, you can send a birthday card or insert a thank you note in a customer's package. There are many ways to encourage your customers lifetime loyalty. You just have to be willing to make the effort.

Train your staff well - Educate and train them about good customer service. There will be times when you can't directly deal with your customers, and your staff must be able to show them the excellent customer service they deserve.

Always be fair - No request should be too small to be considered, and no customer too insignificant to take care of. Sure, there are certain privileges that VIP customers are entitled to, and other customers are quick to understand. But there are also certain privileges that everyone has the right to enjoy like common courtesy and dedication. Never let your customers think that you're guilty of favoritism!

Make sure you listen - It is crucial that you listen to what your customers have to say. This may be hard when the customer is stubborn and unreasonable. Even if you are unable to resolve the issue, your customers should still put down the phone in a good mood because they knew you cared enough to listen to them without confrontation.

Always keep in mind that your competitors are just waiting to cater to your unsatisfied customers. By providing excellent customer service, your customers will remain loyal and never go astray.

About The Author

Daniella Fairbairn, graduate of Wesleyan University and UMDNJ School of Public Health, is a published author and seminar presenter.

In addition to being a sought-after public speaker, Daniella is an excellent team leader. During her formative years, she functioned as a beneficiary of several non-profit programs, including having served over 10 years as a Girl Scout Volunteer. To this day, Daniella remains passionate about her community and the well-being of others. Her professional and volunteer experiences speak to her unremitting quest for personal development and entrepreneurial freedom.